INTO THE FOREST AND ALL THE WAY THROUGH

A collection of true crime poetry,
of missing and murdered women

by
Cynthia Pelayo

Cynthia Pelayo
Chicago, IL
Visit her website at: www.cinapelayo.com

Editing by Karmen Wells: www.shelfmadecreative.com
Cover by: www.elderlemondesign.net

Title: Into The Forest And All The Way Through
Identifier: ISBN: 978-1-7356936-1-3

Table of Contents

Dear Reader,

I have spent my nights with missing and murdered women, over one hundred of them. I have invited them into my home and my heart. I allowed them to tell me their stories through faded missing person's posters, and websites family members and friends maintain as a memory. These websites serve as a beacon of light, hoping to reach someone in the darkness who is willing to come forward with whatever bit of information may be of use to investigators.

There are women in these pages that represent every state in America. They are infants, little girls, teenagers, adult women, and the elderly. Many were students, or mothers, career women, and dreamers, and in an instant everything went sideways. Many of these cases are unsolved or unresolved. Most of the women in these pages have not been found. There are no remains that can be handed to family for a burial service, or for a final resolution and goodbye. In many cases, the parents of these women died never knowing what happened to their daughters.

For many, there is speculation as to what happened. It is often that the last individual who saw them alive serves as the primary suspect. Some are thought to have unsuspectedly met with serial killers. For others, it is thought boyfriends, husbands, fathers, or another close male knows what happened to them. Of course, there are some cases where these women may genuinely have gotten lost, in oceans, lakes or forests.

Ultimately, we can only speculate what happens when someone goes missing. Sometimes there are clues that were left strewn across crime scenes like breadcrumbs – blood, ropes, abandoned cars, articles of clothing or more. For others, there is no trace of the missing.

It is heartbreaking for the friends and families who have lost these women. The people left behind without answers are very often left broken, living in fear, crushing worry, anxiety, and often unable to continue living a normal life without the woman they so loved. Many of these friends and family are forever tortured with their own thoughts, reliving the day, moment, and minute in which they were alerted to when their loved one went missing, left to wonder what could they have done differently, if anything. This grief, this loss, for those who are missing, is agonizing because for many there will never be answers, just a lifetime of desperate questions.

Before you continue into the forest I leave you with a few more thoughts — we are living with a silent crisis, the crisis of missing and murdered women in our society. There are thousands of missing women in America. There are thousands of women who have been murdered, yet their case has gone ignored, forgotten, cold. For women of color, this is especially an epidemic. Hispanic, Black, Asian, and particularly Native American women go missing at much higher rates than the general population, and someone knows something. I cannot stress this enough — someone knows something. For so many women to go missing each year, year after year, decade after decade means that someone knows something.

We must allow our minds to creep to dark places to imagine what is happening to these girls and women when they are taken. Many are murdered immediately. Many are raped and then murdered. Many are trafficked. This means that we are living among people who kidnap, rape and murder women, and we should be fearful that these predators and killers live among us, next door to us, with us.

For each poem, I have included some basic information regarding the case I have written about, as well as an investigating agency phone number. If you know something, if you heard a family story from long ago that sounds familiar that can be a clue, then call someone.

These women deserve rest and peace, and the people that took them away from us deserve to be punished. I hope that this poetry collection highlights these crimes that are very true, and perhaps can lead to the discovery of some of these women. Also, as of today, the day I am publishing this collection, a long suspected murderer of one of these women has been arrested — a stepfather, a man who was suspected in the murder of his stepdaughter for almost 20 years. Justice sometimes takes time, but it is possible.

Cynthia "Cina" Pelayo

I Am Afraid

Remember Me

Into the forest and all the way through, I ask you to follow
my voice
Across the stream and through the hills, you'll find a copse of
trees
Unknown to many, lost to time, and tucked behind a bare
branch
A ball of twine, a cigarette butt, a crumpled polaroid, you
hear a giggle
The crunch of leaves, and the dread stabs your insides, and
your breath
Oh! Your breath, how your breath catches in your throat, and
you
Fall all the way down, into a hole so long ago hidden there,
and now
You are within the ground, you smell the damp earth and
pain, and
When you hear her voice you spin around and gain all the
terror she holds,
Before you there, a girl who no longer is a girl, a girl who is
bone and moss
Leaves tangled within her eye sockets, stretched down to her
finger bone
Pointing above and pointing you out, and you climb against
the rock
And stone, and she bids you adieu, begging you, pleading
you, to make it
Safe, all the way home

Missing Person Poster

The missing person's poster, it does not have your eyes
Your eyes were in my hands that day, but are not anymore
I spoke to the wind and the trees last night and asked them
If they have seen your face, neither answered, and I knew
Perhaps your lips were pressed together, kissing the golden
Sky, I climbed up stairs, and knocked on doors in hopes
Of finding your voice, but none of the doorknobs turned
And so, the car took me down roads, and avenues, boulevards
Through, places you have skipped and danced, and I reached
My fingertips out into the breeze, hoping to brush against your
Hair, but you were not there and you are not here, and I am
Forgetting to remember your scent, they are forgetting to
Remember your name, so I will walk, and I will climb, and
I will drive, so that your picture does not fade

I Cannot Call You

Before the mobile phone you had to trust that I would follow
my route
In the morning, in the evening, after practice, after work, I
would follow
Unlock the door, re-lock the door, and I would sit and wait
for you.
The Telephone was on the kitchen wall, kitchen counter,
hallway table, waiting
This one and only cord was my only connection to you, to
tell you that I
Am home, I am safe, I am doing my homework, I am
watching television
Phone lines would be cut from the outside, wires yanked,
stripped, ripped
In the house phones would be knocked off their cradle,
smashed, destroyed
Plastic bits, and broken hopes scattered across our floor, and
guts as wires
Hung out there in the open, around me, knowing that any
moment I would
Be as well

I Am Walking, Someone Lurks

The man walks too close behind me
The man across the street stops and smiles
The man in the car drives slowly behind me
The man at the bus stops asks me my name
The man in the grocery store asks where I live
The man at church touches my shoulder
The man at school calls me into his office
The man on the bicycle stops ahead of me
The man in the parking lot asks if I need a ride
The man in the pick-up truck parks in front
The man walks up my steps, knocks on the door
The man peeks in the window, and says
I see you

I Am Missing

A Few Minutes After 1:00 a.m.

Gas stations during road trips
Are in between places, they are
The Bermuda Triangles of our
Roads, points of fatigue, and
Cool air, and yellow headlights
Gasoline pumps, windshields
Caked in flying insects, and oil
Stains. She called. She did call.
Just a few minutes after 1:00 a.m.
Her voice was real, and she was
So close you could feel her arms
Wrap around your shoulders,
See the smile shine on her face
And you could hear her voice
Telling you about that drive. Cell
Phone towers pinged her phone
At 3:36 a.m., opposite direction
Did you become lost? Did the
Road twist and bend, redirecting
You to the remote wooded area
Where they found your car, lodged
In mud, your suitcases, phone,
Tablet, those snacks you purchased
At the station — all as if they had
Never been. Your sister and children
Still remember. Your niece posts
Your face online and tells strangers
That she still prays

Name: Shari Christine Saunders
Missing from: Evergreen, Alabama
Race: White
Age at disappearance: 67
Missing since: 2018

Investigating agency:
Escambia County Sheriff's Office, 251-368-4779

Sour, Patch, Kid

It was close to home
A quick purchase
For candy and soda
When time slipped
Her parents searched
Hours. The police
Called her runaway
Why are so many
Young women of
Color dismissed as
Fleeing from home
And those adults
Not alarmed that
They are not home?
How many hours
Drifted, when they
Could have searched?
How many days
Faded when they
Could have examined
Probed, questioned,
Ransacked the streets
Turned inside out
And within, and now
We don't have a
Witness, nor footage
All we have is an
Empty hole in the
Space where she
Should occupy

Name: Kimberly Nicole Arrington
Missing from: Montgomery, Alabama
Race: Black

Age at disappearance: 16
Missing since: 1998
Investigating agency:
Montgomery Police Department, 334-241-2790

Four Corners

She arrived at her mother's house on a bitter cold day without
a coat
Her mother dressed her, giving her warm clothes for while
she was
Not a little child, she was a child, her child, and in the
contours of the
Face of an older woman, she could see the full, fat cheeks of
her once
Baby, her forever baby, no matter what age, what decade
marker her
Little girl reached. Her sister drove her to a place, and a
crossroads of
Corners, and she was then seen walking toward two men. Did
they
Know each other? Greet each other? Was there fear or joy?
Were they
Friends? You told your father once that you thought someone
was
After you, creeping and lurking. Paranoia manifested to
reality that
Day. Weeks went by. Dirty dishes stacked in your sink. Milk
spoiled
Cheese molded. Organic matter rotting. Your family thought
one day
You would show up, but as the sun rose and moon beamed,
across
Days and months, they knew it was time. They finally
reported you
As missing. They called you trusting, friendly and generous.
Is that
What happened on the day your sister dropped you off? Was
your
Kindness smothered in cruelty? Your daughter calls you
every day,
Very well knowing the ringing will go unanswered

Name: Tracy Lynn Day
Missing from: Juneau, Alaska
Race: Native American, White
Age at disappearance: 43
Missing since: 2019
Investigating agency:
Juneau Police Department, 907-586-0600

Search Continues, Notes From a Blog

August 2012
The family and community request the Alaska Bureau of
Investigation to conduct
A serious investigation into her disappearance from the
Granite Creek Campground
Where she was last seen camping with her boyfriend. He said
she became upset
With him, and walked away into the forest around midnight,
leaving her phone, and
Belongings behind. Her boyfriend did not report her missing
until four days later.

September 2012
The Alaska Bureau of Investigation will now coordinate the
investigation. Family
Members retuned to Granite Creek to continue the search.
Her brother rafted miles.
The helicopter search was postponed due to rain.

October 2012
There will be a coordinated search of the area of the Granite
Creek Campground
Where she was last seen. Her family will search by foot, as
well as via RTV, boat
And air.

November 2012
The 1-501 Infantry heard about her and have volunteered in
the search.

December 2012
She has been missing more than five months now. Her family
continues actively
Searching. Over the course of the search two articles of
clothing were discovered.

2013
Nearly a year since she disappeared. The winter snows have vanished. Her family
Continues the search. Her father can't stop looking.

2014
The family thanks you for your continued search, and to those who keep her
Memory alive. We hope we find her. Also, there has been confusion as to the
Location of the search. Moose Pass and Granite Creek are 33 miles apart.
She disappeared from Granite Creek Campground.

No new blog entry since 2014.

Name: Valerie Jeanette Sifsof
Missing from: Anchorage, Alaska
Race: Native American
Age at disappearance: 43
Missing since: 2012
Investigating agency:
Alaska State Troopers, 907-783-0972

Media Fades With Age, its Disability

Authorities cannot tell us how she died.
No clothing or personal items were found
With the remains. The things they call us
After we were flesh and blood, remains,
What remains. The cause of death then
Documented, written off, as undetermined
A hiker found her a mile away from where
She was last seen, in an area called Picture
Rocks, and how could anyone picture that
Their child would be found as a pile of rubble
Her mother wants to make it very clear, her
Daughter would never wander off to the desert
Alone, a woman almost 40 with the magical
Function of an 8-year-old child, and mother
Was only in the shower for a few minutes and
You were seated out on the front porch, and in
That instant you were gone, but you would never
Just leave home on your own. We can only surmise.
We can only assume. We can only fill in the gaps
Of led astray, and led away.

Name: Sarah Galloway
Remains found in: Pima County, Arizona
Race: White
Age at disappearance: 38
Year discovered: 2020
Case status: Unresolved
Investigating agency:
Pima County Police Department, 520-351-4600

You Have Always Watched Me

Your father claims you are a runaway
We later learned he picked you up
On your last day of days, the next sun
There would be no questions of where
You were. There would be no panic
Surveillance equipment dotted the
House. Cameras spotlighted your life
In your bedroom, and at your job he
Filmed. Soon after you were last seen
Your father sold his two trucks. The
Day you were last seen the surveillance
Equipment in your dwelling failed, for
A man who recorded your every blink
And turn, your every utterance within
Your household, and on the day for you
To disappear, for the devices to die
Would seem coincidental? Suspicious?
He dismissed your abrupt departure as
That of a teen fleeing to California in
Search of sun-kissed dreams. After he
Was released from prison, for offenses
Other than yours he grimaced in your
Sister's face and growled "Be at the
deathbed...I will give you the honest
answers you want to hear"

Name: Alissa Turney
Missing from: Phoenix, Arizona
Race: White
Age at disappearance: 17
Missing since: 2001
Investigating agency:
Phoenix Police Department, 602-262-6011

The Sun Rises in the Night

She left work at the time many awake, as the sun rises,
And light enters. She was dropped off at a corner by a
Co-worker and a month later her abandoned car was
Found parked outside of an adult bookstore, lights
Empty and silent. A day before she was last seen she
Told her mother she might be pregnant, that her husband
Would be displeased. A small son was all they had and
All he wanted and nothing more. Everything was left
Behind, including that son. His own father abandoned
Him just two years later, fleeing the country, deserting
The memory of a wife who worked when all of us were
Sleeping, and who disintegrated into the glorious golden
Morning rays when all of our eyes opened

Name: Lisa Dianne Jameson
Missing from: Chandler, Arizona
Race: Black
Age at disappearance: 23
Missing since: 1991
Investigating agency:
Gilbert Police Department, 480-508-6500

The Undoing of a Future Doctor

The job was clerical, supporting the
Doctor's in-home daycare centers
After work, your family would pick
You up, that night your mother fell
Asleep, and in that sleep she awoke
To a new life, missing your scheduled
Pick-up, and he said you left home
On your own at 8:30 p.m. but your
Mother knew, all mothers know
The movements of their children, their
Mirrored movements play out within
Just thirty minutes later they called
Police who refused to search for you
An adult, they said, who had every
Right to vanish, eaten up into a pit
Refusing you as a missing person
For a day and a night, they waited,
They wait still, another day, another
Night, the doctor refused a polygraph
Do the police find that refusal odd?
Nearly twenty years later, almost
Two decades it took for them to
Excavate, break, tear, and search the
Walls in his home. Of course, it all
Tested negative, seventeen years is
Enough time to clean up any speck
Of blood, and undo all evidence of
A crime

Name: Cleashindra Denise Hall
Missing from: Pine Bluff, Arkansas
Race: Black
Age at disappearance: 18
Missing since: 1994

Investigating agency:
Pine Bluff Police Department, 870-543-5111

Far From Malibu Along the Canyon Road

Patrons at the restaurant said she was acting erratically
The server said she refused to pay her bill, her wallet
Was later found in her car. The police came, and she was
Held for a few hours, released into a blank morning
Her remains were found a year later, among broken
Branches and limbs, damp earth, and we are left with
Questions that mount within our throats of why you
Were left to walk outside of a police station, confused
And alone, who led you away from your family and
Your life, folded in a creek bed, mummified, screams
Were heard there just days after you went missing,
Evidence tampered, bones recovered, why did deputies
Remove you before a coroner, officials arrived? Dismay
On the scene, and weather-worn and ripped clothes
Strewn about, no one thought to check the secluded
Ranch nearby known for producing pornography, graffiti
Freshly used paint cans and brushes were found, offensive
Words of hate and race covered the rocky walls

Name: Mitrice Lavon Richardson
Remains found: Malibu, California
Race: Black
Age at disappearance: 24
Year missing: 2009
Case status: Remains found
Investigating agency:
Los Angeles County Police Department, 818-878-1808

The Demons You Live With

Mom and dad said not to speak or the demons and vampires
Inhabiting us would break through our skin, and take over
The smoke that went into mom and dad's mouth, they spoke
of
Possessions and spirits, cleansed only by a concoction of
bleach
Drank daily, burned back beatings, burnt feet, cigarette
lighters
And visions of a pale little girl on the floor, limp and cold
The twisted sickness of parents who ingested poison, saying
it
Was their children who needed cleaning and not them,
monsters
Addicted to vice, culminated in a closet with a pruning saw
Incinerated in the family's fireplace, remnants scattered
across
The Sacramento River. A year of abuse continued on, and it
was
Not until a teacher found chemical burns on my skin that I
Could finally tell the story of the little sister I had and the
Demons who threw her away and told me never to tell

Name: Alexia Anne Reale
Missing from: Elk Grove, California
Race: Asian, Biracial
Age at disappearance: 5
Missing since: 1997
Investigating agency:
Sacramento County Sheriff's Office, 916-443-4357

Questions Are Not Answers

The vehicle was processed but no indication of a
Crime was found. Isn't the crime that the car
Was found across town from where this young
Mother lived? Isn't the crime that a young
Mother left her house to visit her son who was
Staying with his father, only a few blocks away
And did not return, and has never been seen
Now those three children know the way of
Questions, and the emptiness of answers, and
The disappointment that when the doorbell
Rings or when the phone vibrates in their hand
It is never their mother

Name: Nicholle Rae Torrez
Missing from: Denver, Colorado
Race: Hispanic
Age at disappearance: 27
Missing since: 2006
Investigating agency:
Denver Police Department, 720-913-6911

Conditions Remain, Unrecognizable

Found in the Rainbow Falls Campground
There was no pot of gold at the end of this
Multicolored brilliance, but a woman who
Had died two to three days prior, her head
Split open under the canopy of the Pike
San Isabel National Forest. She was found
Wearing a black short-sleeved Harley
Davidson shirt, and jewelry. The rest of her
Uncovered. Discarded. The necklace that
Hung around her neck, of a black crystal
And a wizard holding a tiger's eye pendant
Some of the powers of the stone are believed
To be the release of fear and anxiety, and
To aid with decisions, discernment and
Understanding. Perhaps this stone released
You of any fear in those last few moments
Of violation, perhaps this stone can radiate
The energy to someone, anyone who can
Unlock the secret of your last moments
You are no longer on the ground, where you
Were cast off with hate. You have been laid
Into the earth, and done so with care, the
Plaque on your pauper's grave reads:
"Jane Doe"

Name: Unknown
Remains found: Douglas County, Colorado
Race: White
Age at disappearance: 13-25
Year discovered: 1993
Case status: Unsolved
Investigating agency:
Federal Bureau of Investigation, 800-634-4097

Your Face is Unrecognizable

Found five days after she
Died floating in a drainage
Ditch behind a department
Store did anyone shopping
For shoes, or shirts, newborn
Baby clothes, or socks, know
Feet away, water full of
Disuse, cradled the nude
Body of a woman wrapped
In tarpaulin, covered in white
Paint? Gagged and bound
With antenna wire which
Wrapped around her neck
Waist, and knees, swimming
In waste, death by suffocation
The only thing on her body
Were silver circlet earrings
Which were unable to ward
Away the monster that killed
Her

Name: Unknown
Remains found: East Haven, Connecticut
Race: White
Age at disappearance: 18-28
Year discovered: 1975
Case status: Unsolved
Investigating agency:
New Haven Police Department, 203-946-6316

Lady of the Lake

One was found with her head severed,
Arms sliced, removed. Floating in the
Columbia, Lady of the Lake, the ruined
Angel, mother and divinity, mother and
Child, and it was your child, your little
Girl, your namesake whom you were last
Seen with, going to the store, just ten
Dollars in your pocket, just enough for
Milk and diapers for your babies, and you
Were seen speaking with him, a former
Boyfriend, a former lover, one time there
Were good times, soft kisses, and hand
Holding, is that why your hands were
Taken? Erase whatever pleasure your
Body once felt? Who do you call when
The person suspected in decapitating your
Mother and severing her arms is a former
Officer? Who can you trust when we still
Search for you in the bottom of the lake?

Name: Rosa "Rosita" Marie Camacho
Missing from: Hartford, Connecticut
Race: Hispanic
Age at disappearance: 4
Missing since: 1997
Investigating agency:
Hartford Police Department, 860-527-6300

Name: Rosa Delgado
Remains found: Hartford, Connecticut
Race: Hispanic
Age at disappearance: 21
Year missing: 1997
Case status: Unsolved

Investigating agency:
Hartford Police Department, 860-527-6300

Peeking Through Miniblinds

Clues left behind: A loaf of bread on the front yard. It had been stomped
On; a pack of Newport cigarettes; flip flops near the front door of the home;
An unopened condom on a chair on the front porch. A witness contacted the
Police, but not until a half-day later. He peeked out his window and saw a man
Dragging you into your car at four in the morning, but thought nothing of it.
Maybe you were sick and being taken to the hospital, he thought? When he
Walked outside to check you were forever gone. He dismissed the thought,
And so what good is checking on your neighbors if you are unwilling to save
Them? Your mother and children have quiet celebrations to commemorate the
Day of your birth.

Name: Nefertiri Trader
Missing from: New Castle, Delaware
Race: Black
Age at disappearance: 33
Missing since: 2014
Investigating agency:
New Castle County, 302-395-2781

A Trip Abroad

The warning was there
A man was following, stalking
Too close. Then, there was a
Husband, marriage troubled,
His convictions in Massachusetts,
New Hampshire, of transporting
Explosives. Who needs to steal
Twenty pounds of C4? Missing
Under suspicious circumstances
A passport left behind, and a visa
Unable to return home to South
Korea if you are being stalked, and
If someone is holding a match to
Strings that explode, are they
Truly innocent?

Name: Song Im Joseph
Missing from: Rehoboth Beach, Delaware
Race: Asian
Age at disappearance: 20
Missing since: 1975
Investigating agency:
Delaware State Police, 302-739-5901

Sheltered Less Than Home

He bought you gifts,
A tablet and manicures
You spent time alone
With this god-daddy
As you called him, he
Never interacted with
The boys, at the shelter
Where you stayed had
Strict rules, fraternize
And lose your job, but
He was not disciplined
Social workers from
School asked thirty days
Later where you were
Thirty days floated by
And no one thought to
See your face, absences
Were excused, fabricated
Tainted, he shot his wife
In those days, and bought
42-gallon trash bags and
Lime. To waste away, soft
Police discovered his body
Slumped in the garden in
Kenilworth Park, the gun
Used to silence his wife
Now silenced him, recoil
Your image last captured
On a hotel camera

Name: Relisha Tenau Rudd
Missing from: Washington, D.C.
Race: Black
Age at disappearance: 8

Missing since: 2014
Investigating agency:
Metropolitan Police Department, 202-265-9100

You Are Not Looking, I Am Right Here

In a shallow grave. Your skin smelled of oranges, bright
And warmed by the sun, streaks of luminous hair
Blemished by earth, tainted by the touch of someone
Who did not love you. The medical examiner could
Not find you, within your breaks, and so thought both
Were separate, the missing and the murdered. You
Skipped school that day for the beach, and no young
Girl should be rewarded with terror in search of adventure
For twenty-seven years you were one of many, Jane Does
Missing. Persons. Pictures. Posters. On walls lined. In
Databases cold. In cabinets. Yellowing pages of dried ink.
Have you seen her? Tell me have you seen her? Almost
Thirty years is a long time to wait. Your mother died
After twenty-two years of waiting. And when police
Officers finally approached the man suspected in your
Murder, in the murder of Elizabeth, and Tammy and Mary,
And Rosario, and many more — he killed himself, because
That is what cowards do.

Name: Colleen Emily Orsborn
Remains found: Daytona Beach, Florida
Race: White
Age at disappearance: 15
Year missing: 1984
Case status: Remains found, unresolved
Investigating agency:
Daytona Police Department, 386-671-5100

Activist

She warned us
Many of them
Have warned us
Many of us
Have ignored
Them, for last
Seen alive, no
Indication of
Foul play, you
Played, we
Delayed, and
She used her
Voice, as an
Activist, to fight
For us, with us
How much
Time do we
Have to wait
Until, we kick
In doors and
See, see, see
She left the
Warning for
All of us to
Read, Mid-
40s, lives in
A gray painted
Duplex, drives
White, clean
Silverado, and
In that house
Is where she
Was found, and
In that car
She was taken

Name: Oluwatoyin Salau
Remains found: Tallahassee, Florida
Race: Black
Age at disappearance: 19
Year missing: 2020
Case status: Pending
Investigating agency:
Tallahassee Police Department, 850-606-5800

In Town on Business

Utah, was home, but work called her to
Fort Lauderdale, from landlocked state
To a state of despair when her hotel
Room door was found opened, and
She was not there, security cameras
Followed as she walked barefoot
Down the stairs at 2 a.m., no phone and
No purse, just a silent descent, stretched
Two and a half days with no good
Morning text from you, and you were
Found floating, and no one knows why
You left your room that night, and no
One knows how you died. Was it a siren's
Call or a serpent's spell?

Name: Kelly Glover
Remains found: Fort Lauderdale, Florida
Race: White
Age at disappearance: 37
Year missing: 2020
Case status: Unsolved
Investigating agency:
Fort Lauderdale Police Department, 954-828-5700

Unaccounted Time

Two days passed until your mother reported you missing
The hours passed like water, and she assumed you were
About your day, dropping off your boyfriend, getting to
Work and back, your days and nights not crossing, but two
Days was too much, and your car was found parked and
Locked outside of a Days Inn Hotel. There are cruel and
pained
Rumors two years after you were last seen, an anonymous
Slice of hope, that your body had been buried in the backyard
Of a residence, but you were not there. Should we raise up
All dirt and dried and dead leaves to find you? Or, are you
Somewhere else we have not yet searched, and if so, can you
Help us?

Name: Shanythia Mashelle Greene
Missing from: Pompano Beach, Florida
Race: Black
Age at disappearance: 17
Missing since: 1993
Investigating agency:
Pompano Beach Police Department, 945-786-4200

The City Takes the Girl

Young woman from Aberdeen, South Dakota
Made your way through Minneapolis, highways
Down to Atlanta, Georgia. Spending time,
Cleaning. Searching for big city dreams finding
Yourself stripped in hotels and motels, drifting
Through Gainesville, Georgia to dance beneath
Pulsating lights, to be worshipped. Shattered dreams
Handed from detective to detective, confusion
Split, and your mother's heart cracked when she
Flew to town to search for you, painting your
Face on billboards, begging please find my
Small town girl, wondering if those who know
More have driven past your picture and smiled

Name: Morgan Aryn Bauer
Missing from: Atlanta, Georgia
Race: White
Age at disappearance: 19
Missing since: 2016
Investigating agency:
Atlanta Police Department, 404-658-6666

Don't Leave Me There

Earlier in the day she was out on a visit
With her family, but she did not want to
Return back to that facility, back to that
Place they call a home but is not really a
Home because your daughter is not there
Nor your grandchildren. And so, she walked
Out the front doors, then perhaps along the
Highway, maybe someone picked her up?
Picked her out, continued walking, is still
Walking, various reports have sprung up
Weeds, of seeing the older woman out and
About searching for her family to take her
Back to her real home

Name: Sadie Ruth Edney
Missing from: Augusta, Georgia
Race: Black
Age at disappearance: 75
Missing since: 1992
Investigating agency:
Richmond County Sheriff's Department, 706-821-1080

Cliffs of Hakalau

A quick drive to 7-11
You said you would
Take your daughter,
Boyfriend said she
Should stay. The drive
Was longer than intended
The longest drive, a high
Dive from the cliffs of
Hakalau. The car was
Damaged, crumpled
Bent, and twisted metal
Luminol found no trace
Of blood inside, and
Detectives found no trace
Of you being inside when
The car flew from above
If you did not fall, if
You did not fly, then
Where can you be?

Name: Marlo Keolalani Moku
Missing from: Hilo, Hawaii
Race: Pacific Islander
Age at disappearance: 33
Missing since: 2008
Investigating agency:
Hawaii County Police Department, 808-961-2383

Waves Crashing

The cameras cannot capture all of your movements
Footage shows you getting out of your car and
Walking into the ocean. Nanakuli Beach, it means
"to look at the knee." You were in an area just south
Locals call Zablan. High surf can be found here, between
Two limestone points. The beach does not offer much
Shade. It is hot and dry, and the cameras cannot follow
You everywhere. Images cannot show you graceful
Beneath the water. Were you struggling? Did you swim
To another portion of the beach and emerge there? Did you
Rise from the ocean's surface? Did you break through
The water on the other side? Are you waiting on the
Other side? Was someone else waiting on the other side?

Name: Melissa Estoy
Missing from: Waianae, Hawaii
Race: Biracial, Pacific Islander, White
Age at disappearance: 25
Missing since: 2018
Investigating agency:
Honolulu Police Department, 808-529-3111

Highway Storage

Belongings found in an abandoned house
A jacket found in a home, not your home
Purse, and shoes, an I.D. card found on
The side of U.S. Highway 95. A man from
Circle H Saloon said he gave you a ride,
Dropping you off, still a walking distance
From home. Why would anyone do that?
Why would anyone want that? If I ask you
To take me home, I expect to be taken home
Not dissolved into asphalt where my things
Will be later found, analyzed and interpreted
I should have never become clues for you

Name: Tina Marie Finley
Missing from: Benewah County, Idaho
Race: Native American
Age at disappearance: 25
Missing since: 1988
Investigating agency:
Benewah County Sheriff's Office, 208-245-2555

Pocatello Girls

Tell us about how two girls went
Missing from Pocatello Park forty-two
Years ago this day. Gather around
The campfire of crimes committed
Against children, bodies located an
Hour from home, in a place so remote
Screams were muffled to those dark
Stars. It remains a mystery, they say.
But there is no mystery when someone
Knows, and others won't speak, and
All that is left of this investigation
At one point fit into a slim manila
Envelope, because detectives of the
Past did not seek further, did not track
Down the road of violence for the violated
You won't name suspects. Shame on
Those that cradle those girl's cries in
Their memory. Bookshelves now tell
Of their suffering.

Name: Tina Anderson
Remains found: Oneida County, Idaho
Race: White
Age at disappearance: 12
Year missing: 1978
Investigating agency:
Pocatello Police Department, 208-234-6100

Name: Patricia "Patsy" Campbell
Remains found: Oneida County, Idaho
Race: White
Age at disappearance: 14
Year missing: 1978
Investigating agency:

Pocatello Police Department, 208-234-6100

Princesses of the South Side

Ten-year-old Tionda and three-year-old Diamond
Guardian angels of the South Side of Chicago, little
Princesses whose cheer and joy will remain on our
Blocks, bright colored birthday sprinkles and newly
Wrapped gifts. They were last seen together by the
Neighborhood children, sisters walking hand in hand
Into the never where, into the never land, and never
Have they been seen again, the city yearns to hear
Their childhood laughter, the vibrant chatter of
Them as teens, the confident commands of them as
Young women, for their energy remains, trapped
In this city of concrete, glass, terra-cotta, and steel

Name: Diamond Yvette Bradley
Missing from: Chicago, Illinois
Race: Black
Age at disappearance: 3
Missing since: 2001
Investigating agency:
Chicago Police Department, 312-745-6007

Name: Tionda Z. Bradley
Missing from: Chicago, Illinois
Race: Black
Age at disappearance: 10
Missing since: 2001
Investigating agency:
Chicago Police Department, 312-745-6007

Snow Angel

Since you ran away once before, the police did not begin investigating
Your disappearance until the next day. Far too long, and far too late
Still, you were too sick to go to school, so you stayed in your room,
Comforted by your things. Your stepfather stayed home with you. He
Says you took a nap in the afternoon. He says he went to take the dog for a
Walk, in subzero temperatures, leaving the front door of your home
Unlocked. He says the dog ran off his leash, and he searched for hours
In the freezing cold for the dog. Your sister arrived home at 3:15 p.m.
And could not find you. Your mother arrived home at 5:00 p.m. and could
Not find you. A neighbor returned your dog that evening, finding it shivering
In the Midwestern cold. Disillusioned and disoriented from the blustering
Winds, and the shock of ice your step-father had scratches on his body
He says happened during car repair. The only thing missing from your room,
Other than you, were your bedsheets and pillowcases. Your stepfather failed
The lie detector test in relation to you. In your diary police found, you say
Your stepfather kissed you on the mouth and touched you where he should
Never. The officer involved in arraigning the grand jury was Drew Peterson,
Who was convicted in the murder of his third wife, but says

he does not know
What happened to his missing fourth wife. So many men say
they do not know
What happened to the now missing women who were once
under their care.
Your family moved out of that house, out of that state, your
mother with your
Stepfather still, and in a state where she always supported
that he did not have
Anything to do with the loss of you

Name: Rachel Marie Mellon
Missing from: Bolingbrook, Illinois
Race: Asian
Age at disappearance: 13
Missing since: 1996
Investigating agency:
Bolingbrook Police Department, 630-226-0600

Down the Hill

Free days from school are days made for magic
They are days for friends and sleepovers, and
Spending hours laughing over one another's
Inside jokes, free days from school are for risk
These days are for exploring and adventure, trust
That we will be home on time because tomorrow
There's school, of course, and another day, and we
Did not plan that once we climbed up this bridge
And held out our phones and broadcast to the world
These images we found beautiful that there would
Be someone watching, then us watching him watching
Us, then we turned the phone to him because
Maybe that would ease our tension, maybe he would
Go away, but he did not go away, he pointed, and
Said "Down the bridge" and down the bridge we sure
Did go, and into a sick place we were taken, down
Past our route, and down past our lives, and awful
Things happened there, wrists wrapped, and only
Each other's eyes to look into before we knew we
Were never going back

Name: Abigail "Abby" Williams
Remains found: Delphi, Indiana
Race: White
Age at disappearance: 13
Year missing: 2017
Case status: Unsolved
Investigating agency:
Delphi Indiana Police Department, 765-564-2345

Name: Liberty Rose German
Remains found: Delphi, Indiana
Race: White
Age at disappearance: 14

Year missing: 2017
Case status: Unsolved
Investigating agency:
Delphi Indiana Police Department, 765-564-2345

Timeline of a Disappearance

12:30 a.m.
She leaves her apartment with a friend.
They go to the apartment of another friend.
They meet up with another friend.

1:46 a.m.
She is seen entering a bar with those friends.

2:27 a.m.
She is seen exiting the bar with one of those friends, leaving
behind her cell phone and shoes.
The friend walks her to her apartment.

2:30 a.m.
A witness sees her walking to her apartment, and sees the
evening shinning on her face.
He asks if she is alright, perhaps foretelling, or he foretold,
twisted events to come.

2:48 a.m.
She leaves her apartment.
She enters an alley.

2:51 a.m.
She walks toward an empty lot.
Her keys and purse are found scattered along her route, a feast
for a wolf.
She and a friend arrive at his apartment, both stumbling, and he
sick from the night of consumption.
His roommate asks her to stay the night, for her own safety he
claims, but she wants home.
She departs.

3:30 a.m.
She goes to another apartment, a bruise spotted beneath her eye,

perhaps from a fall or falling. She says she does not know how it
is she came to be injured.
It is fleeting, and the night is an origami figure, a contortionist,
bending into itself.

4:30 a.m.
He reports she left his apartment, and she was last seen barefoot,
in black leggings, a white top at the intersection of deception.
He texts her phone the next morning, and the reply comes from
someone who works at the bar they were at the night before.

Yet, didn't he know she left her belongings behind?

Name: Lauren Spierer
Missing from: Bloomington, Indiana
Race: White
Age at disappearance: 20
Missing since: 2011
Investigating agency:
Bloomington Police Department, 812-339-4477

Waves of Three

One was found in a creek bank off a gravel road, strangled.
Another was found in a ditch north of Waverly, also choked.
The first grew up on a farm, and she loved the Eagles so
much
That she begged her parents on a vacation drive to a stop, to
A corner where they sang, and her voice was carried up to
Clouds, and within those clouds there was never any money
And so she worked, and while she worked as a waitress, and
No matter, it should never matter what a lady does for work,
Here it did matter where she worked, because her parents feel
That your reputation so cradled like glass was shattered, and
That is why people reckon with what happened to you, on the
Day after Thanksgiving, when your mother begged for you
not
To go to work, for a mother's intuition twists like bloody
blades
Within veins, Your family searched fields and nearby
buildings.
But your mother insisted on culverts, and that is where you
were
Later found, black finger nail polish and ID the body, found
Strangled and nude, washed out by the rains of March. A
man
Years later met your family and told them of the men who
took
You, and your family feels guilt and is guilted, because you
worked
Because they could not give you money for college, and that
is no
Reason why your mother later had to scour where your body
was
Found to locate a hairpin that she keeps so close like a child,
and
Your sister cannot live with what happened to you and she
says:

"To imagine this beautiful girl, nude and stuffed in a culvert covered
in mud and leaves, the indignity of it. The man who did this is
walking free, and I can't live with that."

Name: Julia Benning
Remains found: Shell Rock, Iowa
Race: White
Age at disappearance: 18
Year missing: 1975
Case status: Unsolved
Investigating agency:
Iowa Department of Criminal Investigation, 515-725-6010

Name: Marie "Lisa" Peak
Remains found: Bremer County, Iowa
Race: White
Age at disappearance: 19
Year missing:1976
Case status: Unsolved
Investigating agency:
Iowa Department of Criminal Investigation, 515-725-6010

Name: Valerie Klossowsky
Remains found: Bremer Country, Iowa
Race: White
Age at disappearance:14
Year missing: 1971
Case status: Unsolved
Investigating agency:
Iowa Department of Criminal Investigation, 515-725-6010

Iowa State Coed

Daughter, Sister, Friend
Covered with a green coat
In a ditch along a nameless
Country road. A man offered
To drive you from Iowa State
University to the front steps
Of your parent's home in
Evanston. Last seen holding
A suitcase, happy and eager
Another university mate would
Be so kind. Were they a student
Were you targeted? Or, unluckily
Random. Last seen getting into a
Blue Volkswagen. A murder so
Sidetracked, polluted by political
Aspirations, your destruction
Used for elevation, reputation
Tarnished, like dull brass, and
For what? University, life hopes
Dashed. A family horrified and
Traumatized their daughter was
Used and discarded, and her cold
And lonely, terrorized screams
Heard by no one but the empty sky
Overhead. Will you ever talk? Will
Anyone ever talk? Can anyone ever
Tell us what happened, or are those
Lips still frozen tight by deviancy?
Or, are they dead too? It's been fifty
Years now…

Name: Sheila Jean Collins
Remains found: Colo, Iowa
Race: White

Age at disappearance: 19
Year missing: 1968
Case status: Unsolved
Investigating agency:
Iowa Department of Criminal Investigation, 515-725-6010

Sing Us a Lullaby

One month old, and a one-year-old
Did your mother sing you a lullaby?
Mother clothed you, dressed you, and
Took you away in the night to visit with
A friend. No one has seen mother. No one
Has seen you, nor you, and it's been more
Years than mother's age when you all left
Time does that, it continues its slow
Progression, but you cannot do that, you
Are frozen in baby pictures, and are you
With your mother?

Name: Jennifer Dawn Lancaster
Missing from: Topeka, Kansas
Race: White
Age at disappearance: 18
Missing since: 2000
Investigating agency:
Topeka Police Department, 785-368-9400

Name: Sidney Keara Smith
Missing from: Topeka, Kansas
Race: Biracial, Black and White
Age at disappearance: 1 year old
Missing since: 2000
Investigating agency:
Topeka Police Department, 785-368-9400

Name: Monique Rae Smith
Missing from: Topeka, Kansas
Race: Biracial, Black and White
Age at disappearance: 1 month old
Missing since: 2000
Investigating agency:

Topeka Police Department, 785-368-9400

Slept Away

Sleepovers of little girls, include giggles into the night
And in through that night, did someone remove the
Screen, cut, and placed there for protection, carrying
You out into another world, beyond your home, and
Beyond your repair, leaving your sleepover friend, and
Your family to stand there stunned, remnants of the
Frame just feet away from your house and no one
Hearing the wickedness that prowled your perimeter
That night

Name: Beverly Ann Ward
Missing from: Junction City, Kansas
Race: Black
Age at disappearance: 13
Missing since: 1978
Investigating agency:
Junction City Police Department, 785-762-5912

Movement Through a Telescope

Close your eyes, you are sunbathing
Sand beneath your skin, the warmth
Of the sun strikes, grabbing your
Hair, and dragging you away. A
Helpless victim observes, a telescope
That cannot reach. A suspect who
Commits suicide. Another suspect
Prisoned for manslaughter. Uncertainty
Leaves behind a mother fighting
Malfeasance, cover-up, highlighting
Suspects with little connection, and
All we have are bloodstains in a car
Two guns, two knives, a roll of duct
Tape, rubber gloves, a rope, and a
Discarded part of your bathing suit
On the ground

Name: Heather Danyelle Teague
Missing from: Spottsville, Kentucky
Race: White
Age at disappearance: 23
Missing since: 1995
Investigating agency:
Kentucky State Police, 270-826-3312

The Forest Knows Who Did It

Remains found disappeared, but reappears
Are questions, no answers as to what happened
Ten years before, when the clothes were different
And the food was different, and you were different
Because you were here, and now there is a daughter
Who misses her mother, who misses the point in
What was done, as the last person who says
They saw you — their cell phone pinged from just
One-and-a-half-miles from towers where your human
Remains were found in wooded areas that served
As your home for far too long

Name: Paige Johnson
Missing from: Covington, Kentucky
Race: White
Age at disappearance: 17
Found dead: 2010
Investigating agency:
Covington Police Department, 859-292-2222

I Am Coming

The babysitter was waiting for you, you were on your way
Security logs last have you signed into the Airforce base
Where he was stationed, the Ex, of a marriage dotted by
Abuse they call domestic, and there was a child, support
Hearing the next morning, but there was no hearing, there
Was, is, no record of you ever leaving, and your car was
Discovered, abandoned, and on the ramp of the Red River
Staring down the base from just across that river, and then
He was soon after sent abroad, and soon after that he fled,
And soon after that was apprehended, but there was never
Evidence to implicate him, but your parents have your
Little girls now, and while he is not caged, they will fiercely
Protect, and uphold your memory, that of a mother who so
Loved you, and know that really and truly she was on her
Way. Your mother sometimes awakens in the middle of the
Night, thinking she hears you walking in the door. Your mom
Used to tell your children that you were lost, but now they
Say you may not be coming back

Name: Cory Marie Rubio
Missing from: Shreveport, Louisiana
Race: Hispanic
Age at disappearance: 24
Missing since:1999
Investigating agency:
Shreveport Police Department, 318-673-7080

Fields Solve Nothing

Your murder as reality show
Crime scene, crime news, crime
Cruises, but has anyone solved
The crime? We worship the death
On screen, but need to know more
Information, overwhelms about the
Programs, but not about you, who
Were you? Show me more, the fields
The killing fields, where your head
Ached, and your body slumped
Kidnapped and decomposed, human
Fertilizer, harsh isn't it? It's grueling
To think of a beautiful woman, gone
Dead, skull fractured, questions, so
Many questions, but if the questions
Are all answered they cannot profit
From your murder

Name: Eugenie Boisfontaine
Missing from: Iberville Parish, Louisiana
Race: White
Age at disappearance: 34
Missing since: 1997
Investigating agency:
East Baton Rouge Police Department, 225-389-2000

The Guilty Remain Silent

Police have put out another call for help,
Your help, and did she scream help, or
Was she silenced, and this is all awful, in
Knowing a young girl will for eternity
Have her final words trapped in her voice
Box. Investigators interviewed hundreds
Of people they say, searched the homes
Of her acquaintances, they say, but there are
No arrests, and this is open like a festering
Wound that smells of secrets that no one
Wants to Pine Point — Utter

Name: Ashley Ouellette
Remains found: Scarborough, Maine
Race: White
Age at disappearance: 15
Year missing: 1999
Case status: Unsolved
Investigation agency:
Scarborough Police Department, 207-883-6361

Contestant in a Maine Beauty Pageant

It was the night of your Junior Prom
Cancelled because of a teenage fight
With your boyfriend. Instead, you and
Your friend met two other friends, much
Older. There was a party, and moving
You went home, for something, hesitation
Your sister saw you get into his car, the
The man who said he dropped you off
Later that night, down the road from
Home, because you did not want to be
Dropped off so close, and your father
Says you would never, because you
Were scared of the dark, and your father
Does not believe his story. Your mother
Died waiting for him to tell the right
Tale, about the cold and the darkness
And what lies on that five-acre property
That man owns. We all know his name.
We all know he was with you. Your
Father lives in the same house, waiting
For the truth to knock on his door.

Name: Kimberly Ann Moreau
Missing from: Jay, Maine
Race: White
Age at disappearance: 17
Missing since: 1986
Investigating agency:
Maine State Police, 207-743-8282

Abandoned Buildings

Can the ghosts of demolished buildings tell us secrets?
Unlock this; a 12-year-old girl leaves home on her
Bicycle, not wearing her jacket, but the jacket of a friend
Cloaked in things not of her own. Bicycle left behind,
Flat tire, and a mother assuming her little girl was at
The home of an aunt, but there was no family presence
The apartment building where you lived no longer
Exists. Those people no longer live there. Do people
Remember seeing the little girl who sped away, who
Was led away, taken? Can ghosts haunt structures
That live only in our memory?

Name: Melody McKoy
Missing from: Baltimore, Maryland
Race: Black
Age at disappearance: 12
Missing since: 1991
Investigating agency:
Baltimore City Police Department, 443-984-7114

No Success, No Surrender

Last seen leaving the jewelry store
Where you worked. You told your
Co-workers you were going to see
Your estranged husband, bitter custody
Battle bloomed over a three-year-old
Gem at home, never seen again, of
Course the ex-husband, former police
Officer says he has not seen you. Lost
His job after threatening prisoners
Whispers emerged of how he hurt
And abused you, and if there's anyone
Who could know how to spin a lie
How to weave a web, hide a body,
It would be someone who dances
With the law

Name: Bernadette M. Stevenson Caruso
Missing from: Baltimore County, Maryland
Race: White
Age at disappearance: 23
Missing since: 1986
Investigating agency:
Baltimore County Police Department, 410-887-3943

Riding With Devils

You exited feet first from the
Passenger window striking
Concrete, risking, dying to
Escape the person beside you
Did you fall like Alice, or were
You pushed? Out of the vehicle
Speeding, moving erratically
Trying to dislodge a frightened girl
School counselors consoled your
Classmates, but there is no one
To comfort those commuters who
Watched in hopeless horror, who
Could not save a girl, who gasped
For a few moments out on the road
Battered and destroyed, but freed
From the menace behind the wheel
Of that car

Name: Ashley Turniak
Remains found: Agawam, Massachusetts
Race: White
Age at disappearance: 17
Year missing: 1998
Case status: Unsolved
Investigating agency:
Agawam Police Department, 413-786-4767

Silence Within Your Walls

We claim her, our Dorchester Jane Doe
Found stuffed in a chimney, and covered
In soot. You lay in that confined space for
Who knows how many years, yourself
Deteriorating, surrounded by brick, but
One day the access door was unlocked,
And the chimney sweep entered, and he
Discovered your cradled bones, alone
For so long, but yet not alone, as there
Were people who lived in that apartment
Building for years who did not know
Of her suffering in silence, neighbor

Name: Dorchester Jane Doe
Remains found: Dorchester, Massachusetts
Race: White or Hispanic
Age at disappearance: 25-35
Year discovered: 2005
Case status: Unsolved
Investigating agency:
Massachusetts Office of the Chief Medical Examiner, 617-267-6767

The Things of Childhood

We should live in a world
Where children can play
Outside, in front yards,
Grass, sidewalks, oak leaves
Pasted on paper, proudly
By your little fingers, and
Neighbors say that you
Often played outside alone
That you said mother would
Lock you out if you were
Bad, and what's sad is the
Sight of a discarded bicycle
Rejected, forgotten, a history
Covered in abuse touched
In bath water, lying sweet
And rotten like a bruised
Banana peeled, white tank
Top, floral print pink tied
Died short sneakers, light
Outside speaking to the man
In the red or brown car whom
You told your brother was
The new friend you made

Name: Brittney Ann Beers
Missing from: Sturgis, Michigan
Race: White
Age at disappearance: 6
Missing since: 1997
Investigating agency:
Sturgis Police Department, 269-651-3231

Gas Station Light

Before the drops of blood
Outside the gas station
There was a son, and
An engagement, she
Would never willingly
Leave either of them
Behind, a little boy in
Shorts looking out from
A window pane, saying
"My mom's at some-
Where" and he too
Will know the pain that
She is somewhere, and
It is neither here nor there
Flitting under gas station
Lights, the smell of gasoline
Cool spring air, and head
Lights just out there, so
Close, and she was at work
And mommy was supposed
To be home by now, but
Awful things swim in the
Trunks of cars of strangers
Syringes in a black box
Concealed, stranger found
Jury deliberated his depravity
Less than two hours, but
With that sick stained smirk
He still refuses to tell a boy
Where's his mommy's
Somewhere

Name: Jessica Heeringa
Missing from: Norton Shores, Michigan

Race: White
Age at disappearance: 25
Missing since: 2013
Investigating agency:
Norton Shores Police Department, 231-722-7463

The Trust of Friends

He told the girl he was holding against her will
"She entered my business and never came out."
Was that you? Your friend told you he was hiring
A small paint supply and carpentry business on
Iroquois. When you left home that night you told
Your brother "If I don't come back, come and look
For me." You were last seen. He however was seen
And known for violence, verbal and physical, threats
Of rape, charged with kidnapping, stalking, possession
He is uncooperative when your name is mentioned
He has a lawyer. Your friend, the one who took you
To him, who told you he would give you a job, she
Too has obtained a lawyer, she too remains silent
Some friends open the doors to our exit

Name: Hang Lee
Missing from: St. Paul, Minnesota
Race: Asian
Age at disappearance: 17
Missing since: 1993
Investigating agency:
St. Paul Police Department, 651-292-3646

Dusted Off Retirement

Maps and old year books
Years living in notebooks,
Folders, details of a young
Woman you never knew, but
You called her a "tough gal"
A "hard-nosed" gal, perhaps
She speaks to you from the
Dusted memories of those
Documents you hold, of that
Photograph you study, and
They call you, people who
Knew her, who recall hearing
The tale of the popular
Hairstylist who went out one
Night, never returned to her
Business, and those who can
Recall, have aged now, like
Your yellowed pages, some are
90, and some edge near the
Abyss, and they ask you
Detective, to find who left
Our girl out on the street cold

Name: JoAnn Bontjes
Remains found: Martin County, Minneapolis Minnesota
Race: White
Age at disappearance: 21
Year missing: 1975
Case status: Unsolved
Investigating agency:
Martin County Sheriff's Department, 507-238-4481

Unlucky Seven

Children have arguments with their parents
That's what they do, but sometimes a child
Heads out the door in that anger, and fades
Into a memory. Grandmother and grand
Father's house waited, but you were last
Seen walking, a little girl alone. Seven years
Is seven lucky? There is no luck in that years
Keep drifting, and your teddy bear can't be
Found

Name: Daffany Sherika Tullos
Missing from: Jackson, Mississippi
Race: Black
Age at disappearance: 7
Missing since: 1988
Investigating agency:
Jackson Police Department, 601-960-1234

Silent Car Engine

A mother drops her children off at the pool
On a summer day, a son who shines, and a
Daughter who radiates of cool evening breeze
With dreams of a place states away, slips into
A car of promises turned sour and sharp, he
Was tortured in jail by images of something
Haunting, refusals to speak on bitter tongue
Of inexplicable things that dance behind his
Eyes

Name: Ashley Renee Martinez
Missing from: Saint Joseph, Missouri
Race: White
Age at disappearance: 15
Missing since: 2004
Investigating agency:
Saint Joseph Police Department, 816-271-4777

Doe-Eyed

The littlest doe, doe-eyed, Jane
Doe. I want to paint your nails,
Red, but not the red that stains
Your cream-colored knit sweater
I want to play dollhouse with
You, but not the moldy, brutal
Mildewed house whose basement
You were found. I want to comb
Your hair, your beautiful hair, I
Can only imagine it was smooth
As a spider web, but only those
Insects know where your face is
Now, as that was missing when
They found, you there

Name: Jane Doe
Remains found: St. Louis, Missouri
Race: Black
Age at disappearance: 8-11
Year discovered: 1983
Case status: Unsolved
Investigating agency:
St. Louis Police Department, 314-444-0100

What Amount is Enough?

Will the reward even sway them?
They who know something, who
Can sway this all into a picture
A $10,000 reward. Is that enough
For information of what happened
On a day so long ago, and her tribe,
Family, hopes. Your grandmother
Says she just does not understand
How anyone can disappear and
How no one can see, but we should
See that there are two tragedies, that
In you missing, and that in the evil
Who refuses to talk for they, hidden
Would rather protect the trafficker

Name: Jermain Austin Charlo
Missing from: Missoula, Montana
Race: Native American
Age at disappearance: 23
Missing since: 2018
Investigating agency:
Missoula Police Department, 406-552-6300

A Young Woman Vanishes, The Police Can't Find Her

The reservation spans 1.5 million acres
Your sister stands shouting your name,
Carried across blades of grass and tree
Tops, over a dozen rumors, reliable,
Unreliable as to where you are, where
Have you been? Every time they go search
It's a group of different people, who is
Available, who has the time. The leads
Come, and they are just terrible, you
End of the search. It pains your sister
To think of you out there in the mountains
She does not want to find you in the
Mountains, but if she does she will
Bring you home. Sisters who grew up
Wrangling horses, shoveling snow, and
Chopping wood, now one sister walks
Fearful, yet hopeful, of what the expansive
Reservation blanketed in rumors has to
Show

Name: Ashley Mariah Loring
Missing from: Browning, Montana
Race: Native American
Age at disappearance: 20
Missing since: 2017
Investigating agency:
Blackfeet Police Department, 406-338-4000

Brazilian Missionaries

Your son's remains were found near where you both
Were thrown away, in the Missouri River. After they
Beat your husband to death in front of you, they dragged
You and your son and hung you both. You were all so far
From home, leaving your Brazilian town to establish a
Church, a holy place of worship, contemplation, reflection
Did you see your reflection in the glass when they placed
Their hands on him? A family annihilated for $4,000
Used to pay for food and clothes, by those who said you
Did not pay them enough. Are they paying enough now?
How far can bones travel down river until they turn
Around?

Name: Jacqueline Szczepanik
Missing from: Omaha, Nebraska
Race: Hispanic
Age at disappearance: 43
Missing since: 2009
Investigating agency:
Omaha Police Department, 402-444-5600

Why Didn't Anyone Walk You Home?

You got in a fight with your best friend
And told to leave. You left the party,
Leaving behind your coat and purse, on
A frigid night. Was there intent or force
To leave? Walking through campus, back
To your dormitory, text a friend at 3:00 a.m.
You were lost and did not know where to
Find yourself, and so the night moved on
Smelling of sour beer, and tasting of bitter
Tequila. A person you went on a date with
Once, just once, is said to have said you
Agreed to do things, assume things, all in
Trying to wrap the case around you, but
He was tried and he was convicted and we
Know he murdered you, but all that we have
Are tire tracks leading down the river bank

Name: Tyler Marie Thomas
Missing from: Peru, Nebraska
Race: Black
Age at disappearance: 19
Missing since: 2010
Investigating agency:
Nemaha County Sheriff's Office, 402-274-3139

All Questions, No Answers

The theories and suspicions abound
Internet pages, documentary shows
Reports, and over reports of the girl
Who set forth the first steps in her
Own mystery. The first steps begin:
Withdraw money from bank. Email
Professors of a death in the family.
Second step is always unexpected: A
One car accident, you told a witness
You did not need assistance, but when
Assistance arrived you were not there
Tracks unseen in snow and your scent
Lost 100 yards away from the damage
And when inquiries were made about
The death in the family, there was none
You started the questions, but who has
All of the answers?

Name: Maura Murray
Missing from: Haverhill, New Hampshire
Race: White
Age at disappearance: 21
Missing since: 2004
Investigating agency:
Haverhill Police Department, 603-787-2222

Look Alike

Six weeks before there was Laureen Rahn
Six weeks after there was you, both similar
In appearance, but over a decade apart in
Age, together but separate, and no one
Knows where, the older left to go to a party
The younger was at home with friends,
Junior high sleep overs, up late whispering,
Boys and drinking, but when mom got
Home there were darkened hallways
Lightbulbs unscrewed, a back door left
Wide open, and then mom went to sleep
Because she thought she saw you in bed,
But when she woke up in the morning it
Was your girlfriend, and not you, under
Those covers, how they always assume,
A young girl is a runaway, suspicious
Calls came for years, of silence on the
Other end, and questions of motels
Across the country, dot lines of vice
But no one wants to talk about how a
Serial killer was living nearby, so bye
As he died and took so much with him

Name: Denise Ann Daneault
Missing from: Manchester, New Hampshire
Race: White
Age at disappearance: 25
Missing since: 1980
Investigating agency:
Manchester Police Department, 603-668-8711

Name: Laureen Ann Rahn
Missing from: Manchester, New Hampshire
Race: White

Age at disappearance: 14
Missing since: 1980
Investigating agency:
Manchester Police Department, 603-668-8711

The Newspaper Bleeds

It was a different time, when weddings, and births, and
movements were
Announced in newspapers, and newspapers, remember those
with ads that
Read: "BABYSITTER - Experienced. Teen girls. Love kids.
Work at your
house." Your friend called, but her parents were
uncomfortable with her
Working so far from home. You called, and you were offered
the job.
Your father even spoke with him, adding a level of comfort
to send his
Teenage daughter off to her independence. The man called
himself
John Marshall. It was your brother who waited with you at
the bus stop,
On your first day of work, and on your last day, when your
parents called
John Marshall when you did not arrive home the empty call
rang outside
A grocery store pay phone, and the cold terror seeped in, that
there was
No job, and there was no John Marshall, and there was no
little boy for
You to babysit. Your parents are now deceased, but you are
still cold

Name: Margaret Ellen Fox
Missing from: Burlington, New Jersey
Race: White
Age at disappearance: 14
Missing since: 1974
Investigating agency:
Burlington Police Department, 609-386-3300

Day at the Park

People send your family messages
Claiming they see visions, and a
Payment can show where you are
located. There are cryptic letters
That taunt those close to your family
With names, and dates, locations to
Search, but searches find the empty
Sick vessels of games, ransom requests
You had ice cream just moments before
At a park, at the playground with your
Brother, found crying on the ground
That someone had taken you while
Your mother was seated in a car just
A few yards away

Name: Dulce Maria Alavez
Missing from: Bridgeton, New Jersey
Race: Hispanic
Age at disappearance: 5
Missing since: 2019
Investigating agency:
Bridgeton Police Department, 856-451-0033

Mother of Magic

Your children said you had the intensity
Of an amusement park, singing and
Swinging them, making homemade
Tortillas, and writing them love letters
Your own father, a private investigator
Could find almost any brilliant star
But he could not spot yours in the dark
Sky, when you decided not to wait, and
Instead walk, maybe hitchhiked into a
Constellation

Name: Beatrice Marie Lopez Cubelos
Missing from: Albuquerque, New Mexico
Race: Hispanic
Age at disappearance: 38
Missing since: 1989
Investigating agency:
Albuquerque Police Department, 505-924-6093

The Photo Gave Hope

Young rider, of conspiracy theory
The truck that followed, or boys
That struck, just a morning, that
Morning, and we mourn that you
Never returned from your bike ride
A route you rode on so many days
Often with your own mother, your
Mother stopped riding, for she was
Stalked, and fear bathed her cold
If I am not home by noon, come
Get me mom, and she was not along
That route, nor her bike, but shattered
Pieces of a Walkman, and a cassette
Tape, and nothing was seen, but then
There was that light blue 1953 Ford
Camper shell, and a 1989 Polaroid
Found states away, and is that you?
Developed on chemical and filmed
After you evaporated here

Name: Tara Leigh Calico
Missing from: Belen, New Mexico
Race: White
Age at disappearance: 19
Missing since: 1988
Investigating agency:
FBI, Albuquerque, New Mexico, 505-224-2000

Home Was So Close

Two months after you disintegrated
Your work place name tag was found
In a visitor's parking lot, faded and
Exposed to time. Just yards away is
The bus stop you should have departed
From and curled into your dorm room
With dreams of a future ignored, and
Found insignificant between, by a
Stalker or that friend who did not check
In on you and would become upset,
Or, was it within that space of Pins or
Keyes, in between steps of transport
And safe haven

Name: Suzanne Gloria Lyall
Missing from: Albany, New York
Race: White
Age at disappearance: 19
Missing since: 1998
Investigating agency:
New York State Police, 519-783-3211

Rock-A-Bye

Newborn baby
Swaddled in
Pink, blue, yellow
Ribbons, cries
Gun pointed
To your mother's
Temple, admired
Your baby in
The nursery, and
Said you were
The prettiest
And the quietest
When you cried
That night, did
You know it was
Not your mother
Who held you?
So many years
Soured baby's
Milk. Are you a
Mother yourself?

Name: Marlene Santana
Missing from: Brooklyn, New York
Race: Hispanic
Age at disappearance: 3 days old
Missing since: 1985
Investigating agency:
New York City Police Department, 646-610-6914

The Story of a Girl

Be careful with arguments, or you'll never see
What is just steps beyond your door, a pool of
Unease, a pit of unknowing, and the final place,
The final time, where you will be seen, so see, a
Story of a girl who argued with her mother, in
A new place called home, that was not her old
Home, states far away, and today what we know
Today all we know is that we do not know all
Some people saw, others do not know, person's
Of interest, details of disappearance, and really
What remains are just disjointed fragments, terrain
Remote, contradictory statements. No activity
On social security, through driver's license search
What do we know if all that we know is that there
Was once a girl, a girl unfound

Name: Shantelle Hudson
Missing from: Dayton, Nevada
Race: Native American
Age at disappearance: 16
Missing since: 1988
Investigating agency:
Lyon County Sheriff's Office, 775-577-5023

She Left the Highway

We don't know what she was thinking
Perhaps she was dreaming of adventure
The days before she left she had read
The Whipping Boy by Sid Fleischman
About a little prince who runs away
To a kingdom full of safety, and yet
There was no shelter there where
You walked. We think you left home
Alone, seeking that magical journey,
Like the children in your book, but
Unlike that child's tale, your tale ends
In sorrow, confusion, last seen walking
Highway 18, perhaps getting into a
Green car, covered in rust and scabs
Days later your Mickey Mouse hair bow
And your pencil were found outside a
Toolshed, later more of your enchantments
Were found scattered miles away from
Home

Name: Asha Jaquilla Degree
Missing from: Shelby, North Carolina
Race: Black
Age at disappearance: 9
Missing since: 2000
Investigating agency:
Cleveland County Sheriff's Office, 704-484-4822

I Am Going For a Walk

More years have slipped by time
Than those years you were with us
The officer tells us he has several
Cases he knows he will remember
Once he retires, and tires, and this
Will be one of them. A 15-year-old
Should take a walk and not be a
Runaway, and if a runaway, they
Should be searched for, for we
Should not dismiss them, they are
Ours, your friends miss you, but
Have carried on, and your family
Misses you, and have stitched
Together an existence with cracks
Progression photos find some but
Not all

Name: Amy Danielle Gibson
Missing from: Greensboro, North Carolina
Race: White
Age at disappearance: 15
Missing since: 1990
Investigating agency:
Greensboro Police Department, 336-373-2222

She Was My Friend

Days went by until your father, or anyone noticed
You were gone, the sweet young woman whose
Thoughts were more like a child, innocent, like honey
A friend from your old town remembers you, and thinks
You said you had a boyfriend, named Todd, but no
One ever met this boyfriend, and it was a man named
Floyd Todd Tapson who preyed on disabled, lace and
Brittle bending, he worked at a home for them, those
People who are special like sea shells, or North Dakota
Sunsets, and maybe you were just looking for warmth
For the fierce winter was weeks away, and you were
Swept away before the snow came

Name: Kristi Lynn Nikle
Missing from: Grand Forks, North Dakota
Race: White
Age at disappearance: 19
Missing since: 1996
Investigating agency:
Federal Bureau of Investigation, 612-376-3200

Not Enough Money to Find You

Searches for your body have been discontinued
Due to financial constraint. What strains is your
Mother dying, knowing all they found of you was
A rope and a cinderblock used to hold you down
In the Sheyenne River. A little girl, rollerblading
With your friend on a late summer evening, going
Into the convenience store with dreams dotted by
Lightening bugs, and your friend made it home and
Watched as you rolled away. A neighbor pulled
You off your feet and into his garage, and did things
No neighbor should ever do. You said you would
Tell and he claims the death was accidental, but if
He had never taken you, if he had never touched you
Then you would be here, and not trapped beneath
A river's current, and he tried to leave, escaping from
Bars and cells, dressing into a new life, recognized
And imprisoned again, but the real prison was the
One your mother lived in until the day she died
Knowing your dreams of summertime sunsets, ice
Cream flavors, and her little girl's laughter rests on
The river bed

Name: Jeanna Dale North
Missing from: Fargo, North Dakota
Race: White
Age at disappearance: 11
Missing since: 1993
Investigating agency:
Fargo Police Department, 701-241-1437

Day at the Office

A cross hung around her neck
Two weeks after she left her car
In the parking lot of her job she
Was supposed to start Bible
College, to learn and hope of
Things beyond the here and now
The doors to the office were locked
The radio was turned on, and all
Indications that you were there
Had been there, hung in the air
Like secrets told between an
Attorney and his client, whose
Secrets you may have overheard
Too loud, both sitting in prison
For convictions. Both your parents
Are deceased. Your father believed
You passed on and ordered his
Despair highlighted in his obituary
Stating you had preceded him in
Death

Name: Cynthia Jane Anderson
Missing from: Toledo, Ohio
Race: White
Age at disappearance: 20
Missing since: 1981
Investigating agency:
Toledo Police Department, 419-245-3151

Messaging You

I am on
My way
I will see
You soon
I'm taking
The bus.
I am on
The bus.
I got off
The bus.
Walking
Almost
There
I
Am...

Name: Le-Shay Monea N'cole Dungey
Missing from: Columbus, Ohio
Race: Black
Age at disappearance: 19
Missing since: 2018
Investigating agency:
Columbus Division of Police, 614-645-4545

She Stands on the Grove

She pleads for you in her searches
Plastering placards around town
Organizing searches, scouring
Fields, and moving a mountain
To drain a pound. We want answers
Your Cherokee Nation, one of
Thousands of activists have stormed
State capitols, flooded social media
Asking what is happening with our
Missing and murdered Indigenous
Women, from the lakes and rivers
Of Alaska to the plains of Oklahoma
A crisis for our women, 145 in OK
Alone, when this many women go
Missing in such a place, someone
Knows something, there are whispers
And looks, nods of knowing, so tell
Me, what happened to her? Shorty
Last seen on a gravel driveway outside
Of her own home. A pastor once told
Her to throw her ballerina flats into the
Fire, told her to not dress like a woman
But she is a woman, she is our woman
She is a missing woman, who was stared
At by her classmates with disdain, sobbed
When that man of god forced her
To throw away her shoes, but after that
Moment of hurt, she was always known
To smile, we smile now, and channel
Your energy, for the greatest pain is
Knowing the attention they deserve has
Too been lost

Name: Aubrey Dameron

Missing from: Grove, Oklahoma
Race: Native American
Age at disappearance: 25
Missing since: 2019
Investigating agency:
Oklahoma State Bureau of Investigation, 918-582-9075

My Valentine

Like mother, like daughter
Daughter went missing four
And a half years to the day
That mother went missing
Mother had just dropped
Off her children with the
Babysitter, planning to watch
A movie with friends, and
Was there a movie? What
Did you watch? Did daughter
Know anything? Mother's
Car was later found stripped,
Abandoned, everything taken
Everything lost. Were there
Valentine's Day hearts, or
Cards the day you left?

Name: Nancy Jean Medina
Missing from: Oklahoma City, Oklahoma
Race: White
Age at disappearance: 36
Missing since: 1984
Investigating agency: Oklahoma City Police Department,
405-232-5311

Name: Meredith Ann Medina
Missing from: Midwest City, Oklahoma
Race: Hispanic
Age at disappearance: 16
Missing since: 1989
Investigating agency:
Midwest City Police Department, 405-739-1388

Blackberry Bushes

She went missing in December, month of snow flakes and
Christmas morning cookies, of gold, red and green wrapped
Gifts, and they found some of her items strewn about some
Rural area where her remains were later found six months
After, and those months before a real estate agent showing a
House saw Allyson's belongings, and maybe it was Allyson
Begging to be found, and she lay there out in the open, under
Sun, moon, and stars through winter and thawed in spring
And grass shot up between her fingers in that time, and rain
Fell on her forehead during that time, the same forehead that
Had received kisses from her mother, and reasonings were
Muddled, boyfriend said he and her went on a hike with
friends
Boyfriend said she got separated, and no they lost each other
Inconsistent reports, fraught with changing timelines, and all
That time she was nearby, yards away from the main road
Among blackberry bushes larger than houses

Name: Allyson Watterson
Remains found: North Plains, Oregon
Race: White
Age at disappearance: 20
Year missing: 2019
Case status: Unsolved
Investigating agency:
North Plains Oregon Police Department, 503-647-2604

Apple of My Eye

Did you take the baby?
The baby was in the car.
Not securely fastened
As there was no car seat
I went fishing with the
Baby, and the baby was
There. I then drove to the
Supermarket, Clyde's
Because it struck me that
I needed an apple. Yes,
That is exactly what I
Needed. I left the baby
In the car. I was gone for
A few minutes, handfuls
Of seconds that fit snuggly
In my palm. When I returned
The baby was gone.
Perhaps she sprouted?
Apple seed. Apple tree.

Name: Annalycia Maria Cruz
Missing from: Chiloquin, Oregon
Race: Hispanic
Age at disappearance: 7 months old
Missing since: 1994
Investigating agency:
Klamath County Sheriff's Office, 503-474-5120

Bitter Home

Mom was not home, and you were at home with
Stepfather, your bruises spread concern among
Friends, skin black and blue, your brother's too
He was not upset when you did not return, didn't
Know your birthday but could recite your weight
And bra size to police. Your mother left him, and he
Left bodies of women, how many more? He died
In prison, and he admitted to your murder, but he
Refused to disclose where you lie, in slumber
Eternity, the cruelest of secrets

Name: Rachanda Lea Pickle
Missing from: Sweet Home, Oregon
Race: White
Age at disappearance: 13
Missing since: 1990
Investigating agency:
Linn County Sheriff's Office, 541-967-3911

Pieces of Information

Last seen sipping tea, your things
Scattered across a bridge, and now
They fill chairs, spread out on floors
Crystal candlelight vigil, flames
Cast shadows across your arts
Fresh cut flowers, so thankful for
Your Breath of Light, missing person
Alert, active investigation, tangible
Hope, last seen, worried about your
Whereabouts, they found shattered
Ceramic, and where have you been
We have your phone. Can you call?

Name: Tonee Turner
Missing from: Pittsburgh, Pennsylvania
Race: Black
Age at disappearance: 22
Missing since: 2019
Investigating agency:
Pittsburgh Bureau of Police, 412-323-7800

He Bought You a Pony

Your sister talks to you on a Facebook Page that
She created in your memory, to keep your picture
Seen, and you probably do not even know what
Facebook is or social media, because your sister
Last saw you 44 years ago, and oh, the world that
You have missed, the moments of family that have
Flown by, and you have missed it all, the laughter
Often trailed off by silence, and tears, there are not
Many pictures of you, and those we have seen are
Black and white, like you existed in an old television
Program, and in that program you went to visit
A horse that was gifted to you by your brother-in-law
And that is the last time you were ever seen, and
I wonder what the cries of horses sound like from
The stables

Name: Edna Christine Thorne
Missing from: Philadelphia, Pennsylvania
Race: White
Age at disappearance: 15
Missing since: 1975
Investigating agency:
Philadelphia Police Department, 215-685-1173

Island Song

Island girls. Blessed by the sun and damned
By everything in between. One aged 12,
Took only her cell phone. Another aged 13
Left her grandparents' home in the night,
She liked to talk in online chatrooms, where
He liked to creep. Another aged 17, what
We know of you is that photos of you were
Discovered buried under his patio in a bag.
Could he no longer stand to look at what he
Had done? Even his brother confirmed he
Knew you. We can assume there are many
More, faces of girls whose photographs will
Never be taken, buried beneath waterfalls
Beaches, watery burials in the Pacific Ocean
We can hear their mourning songs erupt from
The rainforest at night, pleading, come find
Me

Name: Kamyle Stephanie Burgos Ortiz
Missing from: San Lorenzo, Puerto Rico
Race: Hispanic
Age at disappearance: 12
Missing since: 2006
Investigating agency:
Interpol Puerto Rico Office, 787-744-7252

Name: Cristina Ester Ruiz-Rodriguez
Missing from: Guayanilla, Puerto Rico
Race: Hispanic
Age at disappearance:13
Missing since: 2006
Investigating agency:
Interpol Puerto Rico Office, 787-475-4378

Name: Yeritza Aponte-Soto
Missing from: Juana Diaz, Puerto Rico
Race: Hispanic
Age at disappearance:17
Missing since: 2001
Investigating agency:
Interpol Puerto Rico Office, 787-475-4378

Discard the Words

High-risk, that's what police call it when they insinuate
Your murder was meant to be, justified, yet what they
Do not call high-risk, whose life styles they do not question
Are those skilled with the ways of bloodstained bath tubs
Who stab, cut, slice, dislodge. Who trace steps. Track
humans
And carry dismembered parts of a body, wrapped in
Plastic, a present, an offering for dumpsters and landfills
Humans most foul who are unapologetic for those they have
Castaway, whose screams thrilled them and filled them with
Joy, who subsist and sustain themselves on terror, let's bury
The words "high-risk lifestyle" and instead replace them
with
The man who murdered you, a man, who is not just a man, a
Serial killer

Name: Audrey Lynn Harris
Missing from: Woonsocket, Rhode Island
Race: Black
Age at disappearance: 33
Missing since: 2003
Investigating agency:
Woonsocket Police Department, 401-766-1212

Compass

Turtles and a rose, compass tattoo
Can that compass point me in your
Direction? Guardians of the north,
Seekers of the east, south and then
West, the arrows are broken, your
Car was located at Peachtree Boat
Landing along the Waccamaw River
False information posted on social
Media, spinning the direction in
Which we should seek, a husband
And wife were later charged with
Your murder, but he was only then
Sentenced to thirty years, what is
The punishment for a life stolen
From time?

Name: Heather Rachelle Elvis
Missing from: Myrtle Beach, South Carolina
Race: White
Age at disappearance: 20
Missing since: 2013
Investigating agency:
Horry County Police Department, 843-915-5350

Judge Dismisses Murder Charges in Missing Girl's Case

Little girl last seen with her friend. What color are your
Eyes, child? Brown, like an eagle's wings. And what color is
Your hair, my dear? Black like a raven's feather. Tell me
About the rest. Pierced ears. Black shoes. Red purse. A shirt
With black and yellow stripes. It was a day for a trip, a day
For a thrill, and so Sandi and I took to the road, two thumbs
Signaling a journey, shortly after a trucker stopped and
When things stop is when other things start, back to his house
"We're gonna get you guys some food, then take you back to
the
House so you can clean up and eat." Within that house of
terrors
I found beatings and wrists wrapped in coat hangers and duct
Tape. She escaped, half nude and half broken, seeking help
From a neighbor but when the police arrived he and I were
gone
All I can remember are two stuffed animals, a green frog and
a
Pink snake with a bow tie, all of us stuffed in his truck

Name: Sharon Baldeagle
Missing from: Eagle Butte, South Dakota
Race: Native American
Age at disappearance: 12
Missing since: 1984
Investigating agency:
Fall River County Sheriff's Office, 605-745-4444

Shotgun Jane Doe

They picked her up in Greene County
Her, and the two men kicked in the door
Of a house, not theirs, and a shotgun
Blast opened the door, and met her
The two men said they didn't even know
Her name, "Victim had no identification
On her person." Yet, she speaks to us
In clues, brown hair and brown eyes
Miami Dolphins Jersey, and the letters
"BH" tattooed on her upper forearm
Besides the bullet holes that pierce her
Body, the coroner found a life of pain,
Healed clavicle fracture, crushed vertebrae
Metal pins and metal plates, and you
Left behind your metal chain bracelet
And you also left behind your name

Name: Unknown
Remains found: Knox County, Tennessee
Race: White
Age at disappearance: 21 - 30
Year discovered: 1987
Case status: Unsolved
Investigating agency:
Knox County Police Department, 865-922-1070

Imagine the Alternative

Let's imagine a life you would have lived
You were gifted, and talented in music, and
Dance, and swimming. Let's imagine you
An accomplished woman, a healer of people
A developer of ideas, an entrepreneur who
Developed systems of love and peace. Let's then
Imagine that you never left your mother's
House to go to the neighbor's apartment, and in
Those minutes, that spark an undoing, that
You did arrive at that neighbor's house and back
Home, and let's imagine that in another reality
That you are living a life, a full life, a blessed life,
But we know that blessing is a lie that swallowed
You up in that empty space of time

Name: Tasha Shante Wright
Missing from: Dallas, Texas
Race: Black
Age at disappearance: 10
Missing since: 1989
Investigating agency:
Dallas Police Department, 214-670-4426

Private.First.Class

I want my daughter alive, she entered that base alive, and
that's how I
Expect her. Private First, and sexually harassed, not by a
stranger, but
By the commander who was supposed to protect her,
Sergeant called
You in on your day off, why must that be, class, she was all
class, and
She was brave as soldiers are brave, and she was all Texas,
and Lone Star
And so many people needed to shout her name, strangers,
and friends
Mothers, and peers, and why was her barracks cleared out,
and why was
She not present at roll call and you do not think that
suspicious, and
Where is my sister, "How can this happen on a military base?
How can
This happen while she was on duty? How could it just
happen and let it go
Under the rug like it was nothing? They take sexual
harassment, sexual assault
As a joke. Did you see the hashtag 'I am Vanessa Guillen'?
All those men
And women in our service suffering from sexual harassment
suffering from
Sexual assault because they reported it. They take it as a joke.
My sister is no
Joke. My sister is a human being and I want justice. And I
want answers
Because my sister did not do this to herself. Someone did it."
And when
After the uproar, and after the celebrities, and after the
politicians finally
Called her name, and the authorities finally closed in, and

approached the
Commander, the suspect, all snakeskin, reached up, and reached out, and
Shot himself. When the sister was asked if she had ever met the suspect
She said yes, he had laughed at her just days before.

Name: Vanessa Guillen
Remains found: Belton, Texas
Race: Hispanic
Age at disappearance: 20
Year missing: 2020
Case status: Pending conviction

Encased in Amber

Your phone buzzes and blares, because of her, Amber,
The alert framed in the name of a nine-year-old child
Her and her brother rode their bikes in an abandoned
Grocery store parking lot, but her brother rode home
Leaving her in the Arlington, Texas winter day alone,
She was held for days, by a stranger, who later cut and
Discarded her into a creek. Her case remains unsolved
While you may grumble that the sounds of your devices
Blaring a license plate, name of a child, is an inconvenience
To you, I'm sure Amber's mother wishes she had this alert
That maybe if her daughter's disappearance had rang and
Roared in the hands of everyone nearby maybe there
Could have been a sprinkle of a chance that the child she
Carried in her body for nine months, could have been saved
But now her mother is left with the husk of memories, and
The guilt of knowing that last too tight hug was indeed the
End

Name: Amber Rene Hagerman
Remains found: Arlington, Texas
Race: White
Age at disappearance: 9
Year missing: 1996
Case status: Unsolved
Investigating agency:
Arlington Police Department, 817-274-4444

Family Dysfunction

A great American family tragedy,
Of young love, turned putrid and
Foul, a husband who controlled and
A father-in-law who obsessed over
His darling, beautiful daughter-in-law,
Little children too. A late night camping
Trip in the cold and snow, and a little
Boy who told, mommy didn't return
From that trip, and later said mommy
Was dead. When grandma and
Grandpa wanted to take mommy's
Little boys away from daddy, because
There was suspicion of neglect, and
Cruelty, and murder, daddy locked
The doors, raised a hatchet, and set
The house ablaze, with him and his
Two little boys. His brother killed himself
Too, jumping from the roof of his garage
All later learning he had sold his car
Just days after his sister-in-law disappeared
Father-in-law died, and anyone who is
Suspect is now gone and dead, and none
Of the suicide notes mentioned where
Mommy can be found

Name: Susan Marie Cox Powell
Missing from: West Valley City, Utah
Race: White
Age at disappearance: 28
Missing since: 2009
Investigating agency:
West Valley Police Department, 801-963-3462

Victim of America's Serial Killer

Their remains have never been uncovered
Recovered. You cannot rehabilitate a man
Who cannot keep count of how many women
Were tricked, forced into his car, Volkswagen
Strangled, headless, limp bodies to violate and
There's no remorse in dismantling a human body,
Disconnected now from any connection, and hers,
What about her, Ted? First you say no, and then
You said yes, pointing to the Capitol Reef National
Park, over two hundred miles from where she was
Taken, that was a long drive. How far down was she
Buried? The others? Hundreds? Her?

Name: Nancy Wilcox
Missing from: Holladay, Utah
Race: White
Age at disappearance: 16
Missing since: 1974
Investigating agency:
Holladay Police Department, 801-468-2204

We Need to See You

Final moment, leaving a now defunct shopping mall
A fur coat in hand, later found hanging in your closet
In a rented apartment you moved into shortly after
Mother died. Food found burning on the stove, and a
Table set, an uneaten meal, an unworn coat, a woman
Who has no recent photographs, who finished college,
Spent years holding jobs for just a few months aching
To find herself, trying to hold onto the memory of a
Love lost a decade prior, and then with the death of a
Mother came her own loss. How are we supposed to
Locate you if the last picture we have of you is one taken
Sixteen years before you were last seen? What did you
Look like on that day?

Name: Patricia Lee Hesse
Missing from: Rutland, Vermont
Race: White
Age at disappearance: 34
Missing since: 1981
Investigating agency:
Rutland Police Department, 802-773-1816

U.S. Route 29

Charged with abduction, murder
Intent to defile, a beautiful child,
In the trailer they found hair, one
Of your earrings, eyelash extensions
A human fingernail. While he was
Charged with your abduction, we
Still do not have you, and U.S.
Route 29 has seen some things,
Women falling in and falling out
Women found missing, and others
Found dead, the corridor of broken
Women, stalked by stalkers, and
Killers, both serial, and amateur
Later confirmed, never confirmed
Listen to the sound of semitruck
Horns blare as they go by

Name: Alexis Tiara Murphy
Missing from: Shipman, Virginia
Race: Black
Age at disappearance: 17
Missing since: 2013
Investigating agency:
Nelson County Sheriff's Office, 434-263-7050

A Mother Cannot Move On Without You

Both of her children are gone, a son who died,
And you who left a few years before. It's
Difficult for your mother to mourn him, as she
Does not know where you are, what happened
To you. Your mother feels like someone has you
And they won't let you go. Over the years, there
Have been tips that poked. Foul play uttered, an
Informant in prison who stutters, spills his words
Shining hope, of what happened that day, but now
He shuts his mouth. Retracts his statement, and
Says he knows nothing. Why? What is there to
Lose when bars serve as your windows and light,
There is no light that shines in a cell, and why can't
You just tell a mother all of the awful things you
Know

Name: Keeshae Eunique Jacobs
Missing from: Richmond, Virginia
Race: Black
Age at disappearance: 21
Missing since: 2016
Investigating agency:
Richmond Police Department, 804-646-5125

Listen to the Pins Fall

You sometimes hear detectives say
"This could be the lead that might break
This case," but what was broken was that
Night, at New Frontiers Bowling Alley
A crowded place, of pings, and slams
Bowling balls, and soda cans, pizza
And buttered popcorn, and a little
Girl who was led away by a man with
A pockmarked face, and possibly driving
A Grand Am. He bumped into another man,
Slamming into his chest, as he made his way
Away, and it was then this hurt man noticed
The little girl's hand being held and how
She looked different from the man who
Held her, but the witness didn't say anything
Then, or for years, of what he had seen
And then the police came, and then the
Dramatizations came, and then there was
Someone who claimed to see a man
Standing across the street, watching the
Frenzied cameramen, and actors, trying
To get right what had been done, so that
Someone could come forward, with eyes
Stamped with what they had seen that night
Yet, there stood that man across the street
With his pockmarked face, who had already
Been there nights before, searching for a child
The bowling alley was later demolished

Name: Teekah Latres Lewis
Missing from: Tacoma, Washington
Race: Biracial, Black, Native American, White
Age at disappearance: 2
Missing since: 1999

Investigating agency:
Tacoma Police Department, 253-798-4721

Spiritual Journey

She spent her days drinking coffee, writing poetry and
journal entries
In a coffeehouse in the city, her city without a mother or
father, both
Were dead, and college did not lay bare answers, and so a
note was left
For your roommate, in search of adventure — do not come
looking, the
Destination was hiking, outdoors and mountaineering that
Jack Kerouac
Wrote about, in a place hundreds of miles away in Whatcom
County,
Washington, and so you drove with Bea by your side,
meowing her
Kitten song, and you arrived and bought a ticket to see
American Beauty
Then your car was found on a logging road, blankets and
pillows covering
Broken windows, your belongings at the scene, but unseen
was you, did
You leave the mall with that mysterious stranger? Was the
accident staged?
DNA was found years later under the hood of your car, prints
did not
Belong to you, car starter wire cut, and in the trees we can
still hear the
Swaying of the ghosts of your clothes that hung from
branches

Name: Leah Toby Roberts
Missing from: Whatcom County, Washington
Race: White
Age at disappearance: 23
Missing since: 2000

Investigating agency:
Whatcom County Sheriff's Office, 360-676-6650

The Smells of Tires Burning

The car was still smoldering when police discovered it
Just shortly before you were on the phone with mom,
Visiting friends and you said you were on your way home
The last call to the first person. Your phone was shut off
And they should have been shut in, escaped from jail
Across a multi-state spree of crime and rape and death
Alice Donovan, and then there was you, a secluded area
At German Ridge and Haney Branch, near the county
Line. Could screams be heard? Could tears be felt? Held
At gunpoint and what was the point in extinguishing a
Life that was not yours, withdrawing money from ATM
Machines, driving and trying, and finally confessing that
You did kill her, and your apologies smell like the smoke
That erupted from her car that night, and why must you
Ignore our pleas? Please tell us where you placed her?

Name: Samantha Nicole Burns
Missing from: Huntington, West Virginia
Race: White
Age at disappearance: 19
Missing since: 2002
Investigating agency:
West Virginia State Police, 304-528-5555

Belle at the Ball

You were last seen wearing a blue gown, with brown trim,
White flowers, a corsage pinned to your prom dress, stepped
Out for fresh air and slipped. The next morning you were
Scheduled to give your high school's commencement, you
were
Going to be a maid of honor at a wedding, there was so much
Planned for you and you planned, but someone else plotted
To capture you, a living, pinned butterfly, brightly colored
and
Fluttering beneath a hold. Where is that blue ball gown? Do
you
Still dance in it? What was your last song?

Name: Catherine Lynne Sjoberg
Missing from: Concord, Wisconsin
Race: White
Age at disappearance: 16
Missing since: 1974
Investigating agency:
Jefferson County Sheriff's Office, 920-674-7300

Driving Dreams

Four months pregnant
College student on a
Full scholarship, your
Drive for medicine,
Father drove, helpless
When you missed calls
Meetings, appointments
Your car drove 900 miles
Found later, pushed away
Abandoned near a road
And highways, and was
It the highway man who
Had just constructed
Highway 29, do you hear
Us as we roll by?

Name: Amber Lynn Wilde
Missing from: Green Bay, Wisconsin
Race: White
Age at disappearance: 19
Missing since: 1998
Investigating agency:
Green Bay Police Department, 920-448-3221

Step Right Up

You were visiting family, and like many teenagers, maybe you found
It boring to sit among relatives, as they gossiped and laughed, you
Wanted to see a movie, so you took a walk to the local movie theater
Never heard from again, like the three other young girls who left
Around the time you did, sisters in disappearance, of a crime that rings
True. Carlene Brown, Christine "Christy" Ann Gross, and Jayleen Dawn Baker
all disappeared from the Rawlins Fairgrounds, and may have met
With Royal Russell Long who kidnapped Sharon Baldeagle, was charged
With the murders of Cinda Pallett and Charlotte Kinsey, and maybe there
Were others. Yet, he was set free, lack of evidence justice claims. Let's then
Wonder of how many women walked under the fairgrounds and carnival
Lights, night after night, under his depraved eye. Did he take any of them
Out for popcorn and cotton candy? Did he take any of them on the tilt-a-
Whirl? He died in prison, and now no carnival barker can ever announce
His complete and despicable deeds

Name: Deborah Rae Meyer
Missing from: Rawlins, Wyoming
Race: White
Age at disappearance: 14
Missing since: 1974

Investigating agency:
Carbon County Sheriff's Department, 307-324-2776

Tell Me Later What You Saw Up There

Let me sit here, I will rest a while
The breeze is good for me, I'll listen
To the birds, and stretch my arms to
The sky. This is what I need. I will
Sit, and you can go on, climb to the
Top of the mountain, soar to the top
Of the peak, and when you hike
Down, I will be waiting, I will be
Near. You can then tell me of the
Views of Cloud Peak when you see
Me again

Name: Celeste Wyma Hensley Greub
Missing from: Johnson County, Wyoming
Race: White
Age at disappearance: 20
Missing since: 1976
Investigating agency:
Johnson County Sheriff's Office, 307-684-5581

I Am Gone

A Woman of Color Has Gone Missing, in Three Parts

Gone

Is the wait 48 hours
Or 24? Or, do we call
Now, shout her name
Drive through streets
And beg those looking
On, toward our Holy
Guardians, of the
Crossroads, to conjure
Our daughter, sister,
Mother, grandmother,
Newborn infant in
Folds of her hospital
Gown, wedding dress,
School uniform, work
Clothes, where did she
Slip, down the light
Filtered crevice of a
Long forgotten canal
Abandoned gold mines
Radiating heat, but you
Said she was with her
Friend, lover, on her way
Alone, walking down
This single road, and she
Is not here now, and she
Is not calling, and it's
Time to scream her name
Into the universe so that
Her blood may vibrate
With the knowing of
Your longing for her to
Just walk in through that
Front door, of Christmas

Birthdays, graduations
And moments, and you
Praise, each and every
Saint whom your lips
Can utter, and when
You finally make that
Call to the authorities
They tell you to wait

Case

They say she left on her own
She did not leave on her own
They say she will come back
Home, it's been months and
Newspapers won't print her
Name, television won't show
You her face, the internet is
Burgeoning with irrelevance
And yes, detective, I have
Called all of her friends, and
She is not a runaway or any
Of those other names that
Are said to discredit the value
Of their lives, of her life, and
Now it's been years, are you
Still working the case? Maybe
You can tell me anything, it's
Been a decade, and I feel this
Cold pressure in my womb
Where I grew her, did you want
To see a picture of her from
Her graduation? She was so
Beautiful and she was going to
Buy me a house, she always said

"Mommy, I'm going to give
You the stars," and I would say
"No mí hija, tu eres mi estrella"
And now at night when I look
Up into the celestial body of
Creation I only see darkness

Body

You're at a party and your tiá pulls you aside, and tells you how you look so
Much like that one cousin, from that one aunt, from maybe it was from your
Father's side of the family, who went missing so long ago, and they never
Found her body, que pobrecita, and she was going to be a doctora, studying
Late into the night, working into the twilight hours, between school and work
She never slept, and maybe it was her boyfriend, or that other man who eyed
Her that one day on that one block and beeped his horn and drove around back
Through the street just so that he could smile and she said his smile was all
Sharp teeth and blood stains, and that was so long ago we should not talk
About those things, and yes, she was your age, and yes, she was so beautiful
And yes, what a doctor she would have been, and her mother cried every
Night, and they found her mother years after her daughter went missing
Clutching a sun-worn, tear-stained picture of her in her quinceañera dress

Dead on the kitchen floor, her heart split in so many pieces, and there was

No more life worth living when so much had been taken for perhaps just a

Few moments of violation, I can't think about this anymore, so let's have

Another drink, but there's rumors her body was found by a coyote in a canyon

But let's never talk about these things, and forget how scared she might have

Been when she was pulled, pushed into a car, driven someplace that was not

Her home, touched and taken by someone who was not her love, and discarded

Away, fluttering in the wind like prayer flags, her memory now joined

Forever with the missing and murdered, forgotten and ignored, women,

Our women, our little girls

Echo

Listen, you can hear the echo say
I do not want to die this way
I just want to see my mother
I just want to see my father
I want to see my daughter
I just want to see my son
Please, I just want to live
I just want to go home
It hurts, please don't
Please let me go...

ABOUT

Cynthia "Cina" Pelayo is the author of LOTERIA, SANTA MUERTE, THE MISSING, POEMS OF MY NIGHT, and the upcoming CHILDREN OF CHICAGO by Agora/Polis Books. Pelayo is an International Latino Book Award winning author and an Elgin Award nominee. She lives in Chicago with her family.

Made in the USA
Middletown, DE
20 September 2020